PINK RAIN

Dolores V. Randall

Fulton Books
Meadville, PA

Published by Fulton Books 2023

ISBN 979-8-88505-665-6 (paperback)
ISBN 979-8-88505-666-3 (digital)

Printed in the United States of America

CONTENTS

CHAPTER 1

The Family

It is so nice to know that we have families we can count on. Our lives are built on the solid foundations of families because that is where our roots come from. In the beginning of time, families had struggle together in the midst of their trials and tribulations. Everybody had struggle somewhere in their lives, and some had to struggle more than others in the families. There are no perfect families here on earth because every family has their problems. Whenever there is a problem in the family, it's the older ones who step in and fix the problems. The young had to stay in their lane, or they would get run over.

Families are the ones who will stand by your side to make sure that you are cared for, and to prepare you for the things you need to know in life. Who would have thought that the family that you did have would ever leave so suddenly and so quietly? The strength that they carry for everyone in the families was unreal. There were two strong independent women who stood the test of time—Mother Connie and Grandmother Viv. Nobody could knock them down, and they wouldn't get back up. They knew what they liked and what they didn't like. Even though they didn't wear their feelings on their shoulders, nobody would have known it because they kept their heads up to the sky. They will always will be remembered and loved.

As I can remember, Mother Connie and Grandmother Viv had their own unique personalities. However, they both were favorable in my eyes, regardless of their circumstances. They both had their ways of thinking, and doing things like any of us. We have our ways of thinking and doing things differently. There are no two people alike. I have not known of any. Have you?

Mother Connie was a very strong independent woman, because of all of life's disappointments she encountered. She not only had to fight for her children's lives, but she had to fight for her own life as well. The things that Mother Connie had to suffered will blow your mind. I can't even imagine to go through the things she had to go through. That had to been some kind of experience she had to deal with. Mother Connie was a sweet and gentle woman, but please don't get on her last cotton-picking nerves, because she would tell you about it. She would have you, the dog, the cat, and everything in the house jumping. Isn't that what the older people would say, "Don't get on my last cotton-picking nerves?" Mother Connie was a jewel who had so much to offer the world in the short time she was here on this earth. Life's circumstances kept her from reaching all her dreams.

In addition, Mother Connie's character was like the Proverbs 31 woman, of which I had no way of knowing what that meant, until I was grown enough to understand. When you think of that particular passage, it speaks about a self-controlled woman, who was about doing good. It's about a woman who worked with her hands, minded her business, took care of her children, her husband, and her home.

Mother Connie was never married—not that she couldn't get married. It was a choice that she made. She was a good-looking woman, so she could get any man that she wanted. Mother Connie wasn't the fast type of woman, but if she was fast, she was fast enough to get with my father, so I could be born. Hopefully, you will get the message later. She wasn't a loud, boastful person, but she could get loud if she wanted to. Mother Connie kept her dignity and respect. She was a lady whom people respected. She knew that everybody didn't like her, only the friends who loved her. She only had friends who knew and understood her. Those friends of hers were no joke. They would set you straight for one; they didn't play with kids. Don't even think about talking back; they would point you back in the right direction.

Moreover, Mother Connie didn't let any of the naysayers bother her. Mother Connie was headstrong. She wasn't going to allow people to mold her in the way they wanted her to be. She was about doing good for her mother, her brothers, her children, and anyone else who was connected to her. Mother Connie had few friends that she could call her friends. Like any of us, Mother wasn't perfect, and she knew she had to get it together. And in time, she did get herself together.

Mother Connie was also one who worked with her hands. The gifts that she was blessed with inside of her, nothing but death could stop her. Mother Connie used her hands for knitting and crocheting sweaters, hats for infant and adults. She could look at a stitch in a book and start to crochet. Mother Connie could close her eyes and know how many stitches she had put together. There wasn't anything that Mother could not do. Whatever she put her mind to do, she could do it. Mother Connie couldn't work because of her illness.

She made sure brother and I were clean, and we had plenty of food to eat. That wasn't a problem for us. On that note, she had a job by taking care of her kids. Mother Connie didn't work a secular job to get paid. Don't get it twisted; She had money, mind you. It was free money. She couldn't work because she suffered from seizures that didn't go away. Some people who had seizures and outlived it, or the condition just went away. Mother Connie used to have back-to-back seizures, and get back up afterwards and go about her business. I can remember how Mother would have a seizure, and fall down a flight of stairs in our house. She would pick herself up like nothing, and keep it moving.

I am not boasting about Mothers condition because that's no reason to boast. I was scared hoping that Mother wouldn't do that again. She couldn't help herself. I don't know if she knew she was going to pass out. Why would a young like me wants to know? By the way, some seizures were silent, and there were some that caused out-of-control body movement. With that being said, sometimes you can't do anything about it. The person has to go through it, until it passes over. Like Mother, it passed over, until she got herself together.

I remember times when Mother Connie and I would go out—either we ride the bus or the train, and she would have a seizure. The passengers on the train would come to our rescue. While I was sitting next to Connie, I would weep for her because I didn't know what to expect. Then someone would come over to calm me down because I was a hot mess, seeing Mother Connie in that condition.

The ambulance had finally came, and took us to the hospital to work on her. I am not sure if the doctors kept Mother Connie in the hospital overnight or not. All I know was that the creator blessed Mother Connie to live again. In those memorable moments, I can hear Mother Connie say, "Let me live my life the way I want to live it while I have the freedom to do so. I don't know when I am leaving out of here." Mother had those moments that nobody could understand. It's a thing call life.

There were some people who would look at Mother Connie as if something was wrong with her. There wasn't anything wrong with her. She had good sense. The problem with people was that they couldn't understand her because of the sickness she had suffered, or they didn't know her. Could it be that her skin and hair were beautiful? Whatever their problem was, shame on them. Most of the time, I was there with Mother when she passed out, and I had to look at the state that she was in. Despite Mother's conditions, she lived the best of her life.

Mother Connie could go anywhere that she wanted, and please don't question her whereabouts. She would either give you a look that would have you fall to you knees, or she would say what was on her mind. Mother Connie knew that she wasn't in the best of health, but that didn't stop her from living. She didn't allow her circumstances to get her down. When Mother was around people and especially her friends, she would cut up. Mother Connie enjoyed laughing and living her life. When Mother would laugh, the neighbors would laugh along with her. I could hear the neighbors say, "Connie, you are something else." Then I would hear them say, "Connie sure keeps herself clean and her children clean."

After brother and I came into the house from the dirty streets, Grandmother Viv would say to us, "Take off your clothes, and get into the tub." Mind you, brother and I took our baths separately. There's nothing going on but the rent. Mother Connie made sure we took our baths with no ifs, ands, or butts about it, or we wouldn't hear the last of it. If you wanted a good night's sleep, you better do it the right way, or you'll be sleeping on the floor. There is nothing like having a mother and grandmother who can keep order in the house, and that is what they have done.

CHAPTER 2

The Matriarchs

On the other hand, Grandmother was the head of the household. Should I not say anything else? Grandmother Viv was the matriarch of the family, who had to work two jobs because Mother Connie couldn't work. She had to take care of her children. Grandmother Viv had to keep the bills paid and food on the table.

In addition, Grandmother was another artist who knew how to make things with her hands. Grandmother Viv loved to sew and to crochet as well, but her art was in sewing. I can remember these two capes she made for a family member who loved keeping herself looking good when entering into the house of the Lord. I can remember Grandmother Viv making me some clothes and a hat with her touch of design. I didn't know how Grandmother Viv did it, but she would put a few pins in her mouth and not swallow them. I would be so scared for her, and say to her, "Would you please take those pins out your mouth and pin them to the cushion?" She didn't pay me no mind, but kept on doing what she was doing. On that note, the jobs Grandmother Viv worked was doing hair and making clothes. That was her living.

As far as Grandmother Viv's beauty, she was a dark-skinned woman with silky, thick, jet-black hair to her shoulders, and her high cheek bones complemented all the beauty within her. I believed she had some of that Indian stuff in her. Mother Connie, on the other hand, was a light-skinned woman, whose hair was straight black.

There were times she wore her hair pinned up with bangs in the front or her hair down to her face.

Grandmother Viv was about doing good for everyone. Everybody in the neighborhood knew Grandmother who they respected, and she gave the same respect in return. Grandmother Viv didn't tolerate a lot of foolishness. One thing about Grandmother Viv, she was about her family who she loved—her children, her grand-children, and her great-grandchildren that you couldn't count on your fingers. I don't even recall if she showed any favoritism because all of us felt loved. Grandmother Viv wasn't only good at her craft in making clothes or doing hair, she knew how to cook and mind you, she cooked everything from scratch. You better not put your hands in the pot without washing your hands because she would tell you about it.

Another thing about Grandmother Viv was that she didn't bite her tongue when it came to her cooking. Everything she touched was blessed. Grandmother Viv knew how to bake those cakes and pies that would have you put on a hundred pounds for the record. As far as eating her cooking, you find yourself on the floor because the weight of your behind was too big to sit in a chair. It wasn't that our butts were too big, but that other people couldn't hold up. Our kitchen chairs and Grandmother Viv's cooking weren't a good fit for them. No harm done; I'm just keeping it real. So, eating Grandmother Viv's cooking wasn't a good fit for them. After eating her food, Brother Art and I would go back outside, so we can run this food off of us.

Grandmother Viv would also go out of her way to help anybody. I can remember a neighbor from around the corner, calling Grandmother on the phone, and Grandmother dragging me with her to see about them. It was dark at the time. I had no idea what was wrong with the neighbor but Grandmother knew.

Nevertheless, Grandmother Viv was helping this neighbor, and this neighbor had a black cat. It's a saying that black cats are bad luck. Maybe they are. I don't know. One thing I do know that this partic-ular cat was disturbed. While I was sitting waiting for Grandmother Viv, I was playing with this cat, and I didn't think anything of it because we raised black cats in our family, but nothing like this sim-ple cat. This cat bit me on my cheek, and I guess the cat was waiting for the opportunity to attack. I wanted to beat the crap out of this cat so bad, but they ran from me because they knew they were wrong, and I guess they didn't want to take no chances with me. I couldn't wait until Grandmother Viv was finished helping with this neighbor. After she was done, I was so glad to get up out of there. Pray, pray, pray before you go over anybody's house because you don't know what's up in there.

CHAPTER 3

The Gathering

There were times Grandmother likes to have a good time. Can anybody dance like her? Grandmother Viv loved her music, and she loved to dance. Some of Grandmother Viv's favorite music was Ray Charles and Mahalia Jackson, but to top them all, Grandmother would play Mahalia Jackson music like running water out of the faucet. Sometimes, she would play the same song over and over and over, again and again. The family would come over to visit, and Grandmother would put her music on back in the day. It was the 45 RPM records and those big round albums.

When the older ones would get together, they would cut up, and I mean they would cut up. Grandmother Viv would kick her legs up in the air and swing around like she just didn't care. The rapper, Curtis Blow, would say, "These are the breaks. Break it up, break it up, break down," and that was what Grandmother Viv did—she broke it down to the ground. Just don't get in her way because you were headed for a breakdown between her legs.

There were times me, brother, and the cousins would sit and watch and laugh at them because of their movements, and there were times we had to leave the room. It was their time together, and when they would have some family discussions to discussed, the young could not be in the room. It was the adult conversation, and we couldn't be in the room.

In today's society, the story is little bit different. The youth have no respect, or should I say, some of them don't have respect. You can't stereotype all of them. They'll be in your face, and act like they are on your level, while they are still wet behind their ears and popping bubblegum. How many can say you didn't get the look when you were in adult's conversation when you were young? I know I got the look. I don't know if it was the "I like you" or "I don't like you" look.

If you got the look that they don't like you, that means you had to do about-face and take a walk. Enough said, some children will be in the adult's conversations and some adults would talk to the children like they are adults. In their time, the older ones would say, "Get out of the room while we are talking." They didn't hold back on anything they needed to say. They said what they had to say, and that was the end of the discussion.

Mother Connie wasn't the dancing type, but maybe she was. I had never saw her dance. She kept more to herself. Mother Connie liked to be around the family, and she liked the fun times as well. She would stay to herself for one, she was being herself, and she didn't want any bother out of no one. I believed in her quiet moments, Mother was praying to God for help to heal her from this deadly disease. I would look at Mother and see in her eyes that something was wrong. When children are close to their parents, they sense that something is not right. The child can't put their finger on the problem, but they can sense that something is wrong with their parent.

We all know the song that says, "I had some good days, and I had some hills to climb and the rest is history." Mother Connie was going through it all on every side. I would look at this whole craziness, and wondered if it will all go away for her sake. I didn't know a darn thing of what was happening to her, only to see that she wasn't well. If truth be told, it looked as if the whole thing was like a movie, and we are the characters playing the part. Despite her struggles, Mother Connie kept pressing forward and nothing could keep her down.

The family was close to Mother Connie, and we didn't let her out of our sight. We try not to let Mother go far distance. Mother was determined to do what she wanted to do. The love that we shared was bonded. No matter how things seemed to look, the love we had kept us together. Wherever Mother Connie would like to go in the neighborhood, or taking a ride on Septa, there was nothing Grandmother Viv didn't know about. If Mother Connie would have a seizure on the street, Grandmother Viv would get a call that Mother Connie passed out. Sometimes Mother would wonder off somewhere, and Grandmother was worried. She didn't want anything to happen to Mother. Brother and I didn't want anything to happen to her.

I could hear the echoing sound of Grandmothers Viv voice, saying, "I wish Connie let me know where she is going. She knows she have these seizers, and someone can take an advantage of her." Grandmother Viv was scared for Mother Connie, and so was I. Her seizures were probably getting worst. Mother was tired of taking all that medicine. Mother Connie attitude was like, "I am not taking all these pills with these name brands on them."

I know that to be right because the pills that the doctors were giving to Mother was more than enough. Mother Connie wasn't crazy. She knew it was a bit too much for her. Mother Connie put most of the pills all the way back into her dresser drawer. The doctors thought Mother was a fool, but the fool was them. Mother Connie had good sense, and she had to be free, and nobody could keep her down, including her family. Mother Connie did whatever she wanted to do and go wherever she wanted to go. She was fighting for her life, and Mother was going to make sure that she was going to live her life to the fullest. This sickness wasn't going keep her down. She pressed, and she pushed—going to the doctors, visiting family and going on trips, enjoying her neighbors, and doing what she wanted to do.

There were times you didn't know what kind of a day she was having because it wasn't for everyone to know. The expressions on her face could fool you. Grandmother Viv knew Mother wasn't feeling her best, and others in the family knew but didn't say too much, especially her brothers. Mother Connie didn't let everybody in her business, only certain people. I said earlier, Mother Connie had only few friends that she could talk to. They were the ones she could trust.

You can't trust everybody because some people don't have you at their best interest at heart, only for what they can get out of you.

Mother Connie knew who liked her and who didn't like her. On our block, there were few friends that Mother was in company. There were these two brothers who lived up the street on our block, and their mother was the sweetest lady. The son's mother was a fair-skinned woman, and her sons were as well. The neighborhood I lived in was all different shades of colors, and we all liked each other. Their mother and Mother Connie got along very well. The brothers liked Mother and Mother liked the brothers.

I can remember how Mother would talk to anybody who crossed her path. One thing about these brothers was that they must love some liquor because when Mother and I would go up the street, I could smell the liquor before I could even get close to them. Either I had a good sense of direction, or they were just some strong drinkers. That will take you on a spin. Now, that right there is some strong drinking.

Mother Connie would hold my hand real tight, laughing and talking with the brothers. I am so glad she was holding my hands because I didn't want anything jumping off on me. I believe Mother had good intentions but those intensions had to fly away. Both of the brothers like to hug, but I would pull away from them like a champ. I wasn't tolerating that smell on their breath, and it wasn't a pleasant smell at that. How could they get away with that kind of behavior? Don't get it twisted, I am not hating. They could do a little better for themselves than that. I knew Mother Connie was there to protect me, and that she did. I am not sure who was the oldest or the youngest—it didn't matter. All I know was that they both had hairs on their faces. One of them had a white beard, and the other brother had a salt and pepper look, I think.

In addition, I hope Mother Connie didn't think of me having that kind of man in my future life. I don't think so. I love you, Mom, but not today. There is nothing wrong with some hairs on your face because that is a caveman thing but when you soak your face in a barrel of liquor, it causes my light to shed some light on your situation, especially if I see myself entangled in all that, and can't find my way back home. I know I'll be webbing, trying to come out of that one. That is torture. The saying would be something like this, "Don't play me as a fool because I am not a fool. You have to come clean with me. Sister girl, don't play that."

CHAPTER 4

Fun in the Sun

There is nothing like taking a vacation on sunny beach with white sand and the waves roaring in the ocean. As I can recall, every summer Grandmother Viv would take the grandchildren on a trip to Atlantic City. The beach and the boardwalk are where all families like to go to have a vacation. It was always something to do and see. Some of the stuff we saw on the boardwalk should have been against the law to even be on the boardwalk.

Grandmother Viv didn't show any signs of favoritism with any of the grandchildren. If anything, Grandmother Viv was was on Brother Art and I butts more than any of the grandchildren. She wanted to make sure we didn't act like park apes, but we did for the record. How could you not act up because all kids are full of it, and some kids are full of it more than other kids? It is okay because we got it all out of us, and it was such a relief.

Grandmother Viv would get all of us up early in the morning—the sun shining bright through the windows. Along with Mother, Grandmother will be in the kitchen, making sandwiches and frying up some chicken, so we can have something to eat on the bus and on the beach. All of the grandchildren couldn't wait until we got to the beach. Finally, we arrived to the boardwalk, we ran down to the beach like a bunch of wild cats, screaming to the top of our lungs like we had lost our minds. Our little legs were running like midgets.

Grandmother Viv didn't have a problem with us screaming because either she had to get used to it, or she might as well join our screaming team. Mother Connie didn't have too much to say but to be her usual self. The boardwalk was just as fun as the beach. After leaving the beach, Grandmother Viv and Mother Connie would wipe us off because the sand was matted to our hair, arms, legs, and feet.

Meanwhile, one of the grandchildren decided to get lost, and we couldn't go to any of the amusements until we found them. When we finally found them, we were able to go to the amusements. On the boardwalk, they had this room you go in. There were two big jars, and inside the jars were babies. I would have never imagined that they would have these babies in a jar. They looked deformed, which didn't take too much of a liking to my stomach. I had no idea that these babies exist or were born like that. They weren't even fully developed, and I couldn't understand why they had that on the boardwalk. I guess back then it was show and tell.

On the boardwalk, there were tricksters playing tricks, and a man, who believed was the tallest man in the world, walking on stilts as tall as the empire state building. Further down the boardwalk, we walked into this showroom, and this man was explaining to the crowd what was about to happen. Okay, everybody was ready, our eyes were fix, and my heart was pounding like a drum. This woman comes out on stage, the lights flickering real fast. The audience was hearing all this clicking sound. The room was pitch-black and all eyes were piercing on this woman. The man began to talk and the lights started blinking real fast.

On every angle, you begin to see hair growing on this woman. Everyone was in awe with this sight. Then she started to turn into an ape, and the ape started screaming, jumping, and pulling on the bars. Next thing we knew, the ape jumped out into the audience. The people started running over each other. This person fell, and their head got stuck to the floor. People were screaming and hollering. It looked like the ape was targeting us, but the ape was targeting everybody. I couldn't see, why did Grandmother Viv allow us to see this show? I thought apes should be in the zoo. I know it couldn't have been a real ape, but those trick cameras can fool the crap out of you.

Like I said earlier, some things should have been against the law. Grandmother Viv knew what she was doing when she allowed us to go inside to see a show like that. It seems like Grandmother Viv knows how to get your attention when she needed the most. Finally, Grandmother Viv was standing outside laughing her heart out because she has been there and done that.

CHAPTER 5

Back to School

Summer was over, and we had to prepared for school by getting our books and pencils, and the necessities that comes along with school. School should be a fun place to go to learn and enjoy the kids you are to be with, but why do I feel differently? I shouldn't be feeling that my life is going around in circles every time I am going to school. At the end of the day, I shouldn't be running out of school because somebody's son or daughter wants to fight you for no reason. If it was for a reason, it could have been because you look better than them, or their minds were long gone.

Back in the day, all these kids like to do is talk about somebody's mother, or they couldn't wait for you to get out of school so the crazies could jump you. There was this gang called the Tic-tac-toe gang. I have never learned that until I went to this particular school. Now that was some crazy mess there. Before we could even pack our books to be dismissed from school, somebody's child would say, "Y'all better run because the Tic-tac-toe gang is waiting around the corner to mark your faces up with a razor blade."

After the last bell, we all ran out the classroom like we had lost our minds. You would have thought we were running a marathon race; it was that bad. At the time, I didn't know too much about anything. Who knows? They could have been lying. Every day, somebody's child would say the same thing over and over again. The whole time I was in that school, I didn't see no gang around, and I wasn't going to stay around to find out. While the kids were on a thrill ride, scaring the mess out of everybody, I was too busy running out of my shoes to get home. By the time I got home, I was too tired to do homework. I couldn't even do the homework correctly because I was out of it, and my mind and my heart were racing fast.

Furthermore, nobody in their right state of mind is going to hang around, and allow some lunatic to mark up their faces with a razor blade. Mother Connie and Grandmother Viv wasn't falling for that trick. Mother Connie's fist would have been ready in position mode for the jaw bone, and Grandmother Viv's foot would have been in position to kick butt. Either these little people liked you, or they didn't like you.

Nevertheless, I continued to go to school to learn by any means necessary. The teacher that I did have was a no-nonsense teacher. Either you were going to behave yourself or suffered the consequences. Teacher liked to take the class on trips and reminded the class if you do a disappearing act while in public, she was going to show us a thing or two. Believe me she wasn't a teacher of hate. She was a teacher to teach, not to play with you or be your friend. There are some teachers who will show you a side of them that would terrorize you, but this particular teacher was about discipline. You either get the discipline at home or in school. Wherever way you get it, there was no way of getting out of it.

I called her the teacher of the mother love belt and the father love belt. Teacher had two belts in her desk—one was the mother love belt, and other one was the father love belt. She would take the class to the park, and she told us to not wander off on our own, but stay close. Teacher trusted us to be responsible as a class. Oh no, we had to wander off and didn't pay no attention to what teacher said. Now she told us not to wander off on our own because if we wander off, she said, "I am going to give you the mother's love belt, and if you go above and beyond, the father's love belt."

She usually didn't give us the father's love belt. That's only if we really get out of line. It wasn't intentionally that the class wanted to drift off from her sight. I think the class got caught up in the hype of freedom. We didn't listen, and we were telling each other, "I told you don't go that way and this way." It didn't matter. Teacher was upset and told every last person to hold out their hands. We held our hands out, trying to hold back, but she went on with the mother's love belt, until she got to the last person. So, we knew not to test her patience like that again, and I was ever grateful for that teacher who taught me not to disrespect your elders.

Nevertheless, the lesson didn't stop there because I knew I was too young, and had a lot more in life to accomplish. With that being said, Mother Connie paid me a surprise visit at the school. I said earlier that Mother Connie was a sweet and gentle woman and that she was. However, when it came to school, it wasn't about being sweet and gentle anymore.

While, I was doing my thing in the classroom—talking and laughing with the other kids—we were cracking up. Mother Connie was standing in the doorway. I had no idea where this woman came from. It was like she popped up out of nowhere. Maybe the teacher called her up on the phone; I don't know. All I know was that Mother was standing in the doorway, looking at me. Forget about the other kids in the classroom. Mother Connie's eyes were piercing on me.

When Mother was looking in my direction, all I know was that I was about to get hit with a ton of bricks. Mother Connie's eyes wasn't sweet and gentle anymore. She was furious and in rage. The looks on Mother's face was like, "I couldn't finish school because of my sickness, but you have the opportunity to finish school and get an education, and you in school, playing around."

When Mother Connie and the teacher call me up to the front of the classroom, Mother hit me so hard, I spun around like a ballerina, flying in the air. The kids stood up and gave me a standing ovation because they thought I was practicing for the Barny and Bailey circus. That was a trip because little do they know, Mother was kicking my butt left and right. The only thing she didn't do was give me a black eye. I guess Mother's lesson was like, "Stop acting up with these kids that I am not responsible for or else…"

CHAPTER 6

Let the Church Say Amen!

Have you ever been in a situation where you try to stay sleeping through the night but you can't because on a Sunday morning, you hear the tambourines and hands clapping, and the shouting from the people in the storefront church?

There was this church on the corner of my block that loved to shout to the most Holy God. In that church, they would lift up praises to their God. They were serious about their God. Sometimes, me and some of the kids on the block would take a peek in the church to see what they were doing. Next thing I knew, we joined the choir, lifting up our praises to God. While I was in my room, I heard the church people shout, then I would shout. You think they care about how loud they shouted? They didn't have a care in the world. They were getting their deliverance on. They were shouting to their God, to whom all blessing flow.

I had no idea to what that meant. Eventually, it caught up with me. There were other churches in the neighborhood that had fire. The church diagonal from our house was the church Grandmother Viv sent me to. There were churches all around us to keep us safe, praying, and interceding for the neighborhoods. Grandmother Viv made sure I was going to be delivered by whatever means necessary.

The Hair Thing

On Saturdays, Grandmother Viv made sure I kept clean—my hair looking good and smelling fresh—especially if I was ripping up and down the highways and the byways. I guess Grandmother's cleanliness was the closest thing to Godliness. Grandmother Viv would wash my hair with dial soap in this small yellow basin she kept in the bathtub. Grandmother Viv knew I didn't like getting my hair washed because me and the water didn't get along too well in my face. It didn't mean anything to her. She wanted to do what mothers and grandmothers do to take care of their children.

Grandmother Viv knew the importance of keeping clean, especially if you are sitting in church. She didn't want no problems with the church people. There were no ifs, ands, or buts about it. You were going to church. She would say to me, "Come in, and get your hair washed." I would cry so bad because I knew I was about to go under. That crying didn't bother Grandmother Viv. As soon as Grandmother Viv would put my head under the water then, she would take the dial soap to wash my hair. I would scream so loud. The neighbor across from us would say, "Is everything okay over there?"

Grandmother Viv would say, "Oh, everything is okay. I am washing my baby head." What a relief after she was done with my head. I couldn't wait until she was done.

After Grandmother Viv was done washing my hair, she would grease my scalp and hair with the big V05. The next day, which was Sunday, she would get me up to put a hot comb in my hair to straighten my hair and then curl it to give me Shirley temple curls. I don't know what it was with Grandmother Viv and the stove. She loved to fry chicken, while doing my hair. It was a hot mess in the kitchen, but she knew what she was doing. She could fry a chicken. The woman can burn. I wasn't feeling it.

I was hoping between her frying chicken for dinner and doing my hair at the same time, my head wouldn't catch on fire. I knew she wanted to get her cooking on. I didn't need to go to church with a burnt smelly hair dew, not after she put all those curls in my hair, and hoping that we were not going to eat hair chicken for dinner with vegetables.

I was able to put on my white dress, my printed white stockings and my white patent leather shoes. All that white I had to wear to go church just to listen to the sermon, which I don't know what the preacher was saying. I didn't know nothing about ushering nobody nowhere and for no reason. I was like, "Where is my Louis Vuitton and Gucci bag to complete my holistic outfit?"

She would put some money in a handkerchief, so I can put money in the offering plate. I thought the handkerchief was to blow your nose, not put money in it. I would dare not to say that to her because she would have pop me not one or two times, but three or four times. That was my imaginative thought. Putting money in a handkerchief was like taking the money out of the handkerchief and buying some candy at the candy store across the street from the church. I would go to church across the street from our house, and my intention was to buy some candy after church.

While the money plate was being passed around, I put my share of some quarters in the plate after church. I went to the candy store that sold all kinds of penny candies. There was this particular candy that I was in love with and that was the lipstick candy. I am sure everybody knows about the lipstick candy. Oh, I love the red lipstick candy because it was yummy to my tummy. Grandmother Viv didn't bother asking me what I have done with the money. All I know was that I had to get mine. As far as Grandmother Viv was concerned, she sent me to church, and that is all that matters.

Tragedy

Meanwhile, families comes together again to show their love and appreciation for one another. It's not like we see each other every day in the week, only for those who live together, the ones who like to get on each other nerves. I don't have a problem riding Septa, only to know that riding the buses or the trains wasn't as fun for me anymore. Wherever I needed to go, SEPTA was convenient to ride. Sometimes, riding in the car was somewhat nerve-racking because I couldn't barely see out of the window, unless Mother sat me on her lap to look out of the window. Brother Art didn't have too much of a problem seeing out the window because of his lengthy body and his big head.

Mother Connie's way of getting around was to ride the bus or the train. That was the only way she could take care of her business. All of us took the bus or the train to get where we needed to go, unless somebody in the family offered us a ride in their car. There were times I would walk because I didn't have the money to ride the bus, and that was alright with me. Walking kept me in good shape. Most of the time, Grandmother Viv and I would ride the bus or the train to see family. However, I don't recall if someone took us or we took the bus, whichever way we went.

If Grandmother Viv and I had somewhere to go, we didn't have to worry about getting a ride back home. For whatever reason why Mother Connie and Brother Art didn't come, I don't know. The family was glad to see me and Grandmother Viv, and we were glad to see them as well. I was on the porch, talking to the cousins, and the older ones were in the house. You know the saying the young together and the old talking business, cutting up. Grandmother Viv and I stayed for a while. I don't recall how many hours we stayed, but it seemed forever. It was a full house. All I knew was that everybody was in the house. I know Great-grandmother was there and her three daughters, and I was there. It was an army of us.

In addition, it was getting late, and Grandmother Viv and I were ready to go home. You never think anything would happen along the way. Grandmother and I had no thought that anything bad would happen, neither the other family members. We finally left, and one of the aunts was driving and didn't mind taking us home. There were the two aunts in the front of the car, Great-grandmother at the window, Grandmother Viv in the middle, and I wanted to sit at the window.

It seemed that the conversation never ended from the time we left the family house. You know how family likes to chitchat. It's a never-ending conversation with them. I'm sure that this is a love between families. All I could do is listen and shake my head. I was so young but not too young to know their mouths were running a mile away, but anyhow. They still chitchatin' about who and what. I believe there were some intervals between them chitchatin'.

We finally got to the bridge, and I was told we would cross over the bridge towards the zoo. I know this much; we didn't get all the way over the bridge because that's where all the action took place. As we were driving, there was a thump, thump. The car hit something—a rail—and we were zig-zagging across the highway while other car's beam lights were blurring my eyes. What a tragic freak accident, whatever you want to call it. It cost us our lives for the car to flip upside down.

I heard screams of voices. I don't remember me screaming, but those screams sounded like death screams. Oh yeah, we were about to hit the friendly skies without a boarding plane ticket. It would have been free of charge, but that wouldn't be a nice way to go, not after the situation that really went down. Grandmother Viv was holding me real tight—I do remember that. The car landed back on its wheels. After that, we were hanging over the rail down to the Schuylkill River. As I was told that the car was hanging over the railing, some type of lifter had to lift us off the rail, and they told us not to move because if we moved, we were going to fall into the river. What a horrific nightmare that would have been. So, the lifter-lifted us up, and put the car back on its wheels. This was a hellish nightmare. How in the world we went that direction?

When the car hit the rail, the car was hanging over the rail. Freak accidents do happen. We finally went to the hospital. The car was in a total wreck—glass everywhere, blood scattered everywhere. I can recall a man coming over to me and asking me, "Was I okay?"

I don't remember his face clearly, but I remembered concern on his face. He said to me, "You will be alright."

Both aunts were cut up, badly crying, and upset. We were all in a state of shock. Grandmother Viv and Great-grandmother was okay, just a little shook up. It didn't stop there. The accident left some scars for some of us, especially me. The older ones seemed to bounce back on their feet quickly. I had a battle to face with riding SEPTA. After the accident, riding buses, trains, and cars wasn't my forte anymore because of this terrifying accident I was in.

Riding the bus was not important to me anymore, but Mother Connie didn't think so. She made sure any place she had to go-it was going to be on her terms. Mother made it her business that wherever we had to go, via airplane, we were going to get to where we had to go. Everywhere she went, she took me, and it wasn't going to be by foot. When we would go out, I would say to Mother, "Let's walk by foot. We don't have to ride the bus. Come on, Mom. Let's walk. I don't want to ride the bus."

It was so bad that she would pick me up and place my behind on the bus. I finally settled down. This doom's day for me lasted awhile. I didn't know how long, but long enough. Other people had their creative ways to desensitize me. How about that? They didn't think that the accident that I was in was a problem. All I wanted was to walk. It would have been a good exercise for my athlete legs.

Uncle would come over to the house and take me to his home, but that would to put me on the train or bus because there was no other way to go. The car wouldn't have been a good fit for me either. The train that we had to ride wasn't a stylish way to go because the subway was smelly and the train was big and floppy because the wheels were too tiny for the train, and the train looks as if it was going to turn over every time it had to make a turn. It was like we were riding in a hell-bound train that made all this squeaky noise; I had to close my ears.

The underground looked smoky in that dark-looking place we had to ride through. What a nightmare of terror. It felt like I was on a hella coaster ride. Uncle came way across town to come get me, and he took me way back across town where he and his family lived. The family knew I had this issue of riding the bus after all I've been through. It was like bringing more stress on me as I thought. The reality of it all was real. Everything I had to go through in this life, I had to pass the test because I had to get this monkey off my back.

Uncle was determined to keep the fear out of my life, so it wouldn't destroy me. If I didn't have this strong family backbone, I probably would not have to ride the bus or get in a car anymore, even to experience flying in an airplane. For me to get from one destination to the other, I had to trail blaze it on wheels, not that it was going to be an easy road of recovery. Life wouldn't be fun if every time I walk, I'd miss a doctor's appointment, be late for a job interview or work, or miss out on a hot date; and you don't want to miss out on a hot date, especially if it is that special someone who wants to take you on a ride to wonderland. After all that, it would have been my road to recovery.

CHAPTER 7

Take a Good Look

Meanwhile, Mother Connie and I would go out—either to her doctor's appointment or shopping. As I recall, clothing wasn't an issue. We wore whatever we wanted to put on. Everybody in the neighborhood either wore a top or a pair of pants or shorts if it was the summertime. We all were comfortable with each other. Mother Connie would wear a blouse and a pair of pants or a skirt if she wanted to. I would wear a shirt and a pair of pants or pair of shorts.

There were times when we would go out. We liked to be ourselves, and we would put on the clothes that we liked to wear. It wasn't like we were dressing up for a wedding or some extravagant event. We were going out to take care of business. The only time Mother dressed up was when my oldest brother got married. We felt comfortable in our skin. So, I am sure if Mother Connie wanted to dress up, she would, but she was being who she was, herself. It didn't bother her any about how she dressed or looked because she kept herself and me cleaned, and her hair and my hair were done.

While Mother Connie and I were walking, we passed some homes along the way. We walked past this particular house, and there were people standing on the steps. As we passed by them, I heard the slanders and the laughs that came out of the mouths of the critics. I notice they were laughing at Mother, and I turned around to those critics and looked as if to say, "How dare you laugh at my mother and think that you are going to get away with that."

There were no doubt in my mind that Mother Connie didn't hear those critics mocking her, while we walked past them. I know she heard that because I heard it, and we kept it moving. Mother Connie didn't say a mumbling word. Back in the day, when you talk about somebody's mother, it was on like popcorn. Ain't nobody got time for you to be talking down on somebody's mother. You about to get hit with a ton of bricks. So anyway, Mother Connie was a flower that bloomed, and I believe her mission down here on Earth was to be kind to people she come in contact with and take care of her children the best that she knows how—and she did that, and to live as close as she could from the good book. I believed she has done that, as the good Lord requires for her to do. As he did his mission, that was to heal the sick, and to save those people who criticized her.

Mother Connie never worked a day in her life. I was the employment for her. Mother was able to get food stamps and money to keep food in the house, so we could eat, and so Brother Art and I could live a decent life. She knew that she didn't have all that she would like to have, but the little bit that she did have, Mother Connie made much out of it.

There are some families who can never work because of life circumstances. If Mother Connie could work, she would, but because of her illness, it caused her not to work. It's not an excuse but facts, as far as Mother was concerned. Mother Connie was in the system, so she could get the benefits, so her children could eat and be taken care of if we get sick. She knew what she was doing. She had her stuff together.

I saw the tens and the twenty-dollar bills that was put before my eyes. Brother Art and I never felt the depression. Oh yeah! We had food to eat and never had to feel that we were without a meal. Between Grandmother Viv's social security check and Mother Connie's green stamps—Oh yeah! You bet your bottom dollar, we were living like kings and queens.

The Dress-Up

On the other hand, Grandmother Viv was the one who liked to dress up, and there were times she didn't dress up. When Grandmother Viv would go out, she would put on her ruby red lipstick—which would put a flash around her skin tone—and her red nail polish. As I can remember, she loved her Estee Lauder perfume. It was in a brown color bottle with a gold top. I would sit in her room to watch her get dressed with her big round breast sitting on top of her chest.

Now children should be about their own business, but Grandmother Viv's business was my business. Grandmother Viv didn't have a problem showing off her black and beauty because she knew she was built for greatness. She was proud of what she had, and that is why she married that man, and those three kiddies she gave birth to. Enough said about Grandmother's bomb.com because she was the bomb, and she knew it.

Remember those stockings that would go up to your thighs? Well, Grandmother Viv would put on her stockings with the thick elastic band to hold the stockings up. Then, she would put on her black dress that was alluring, and then put on her perfume and sprayed me along with it. It was a reminder to let me know that this is how a lady should smell. The perfume smell so good and strong, it would make your head turn tipsy top.

Grandmother Viv would go out to a family gathering, and she will look sharp in her dress and high-heeled shoes. Her dress would fit her perfect, curvy shape. Grandmother Viv would put on her makeup and jewelry. Then, there were times Grandmother Viv would be her regular self around the house. She would have on her house dress with her clicky clock shoes, walking across the bare floor. When we were downstairs, we could hear Grandmother Viv coming down the stairs, sounding like clicky clock, clicky clock. So if you decided to get into any trouble, just know you have enough time to wrap it up because you know she is coming. Therefore, be on your best behavior because there wasn't anything that she didn't know.

The Hospital Stay

Meanwhile, Mother Connie's health was declining and she was admitted into the hospital for weeks. Grandmother Viv had taken me to see Mother. Hospital visitation wasn't allowed at that time. Children were not allowed on the hospital floor. I guess it was the hospital rules and policies. I was able to see Mother, and she was all smiles, waiting outside of her room for me and Grandmother Viv. Mother Connie was all smiles, waiting outside of her room for me and Grandmother Viv.

Finally, Mother Connie was able to come home from the hospital. I couldn't understand how in the world? Why did the hospital keep Mother for so long? Children need their mother. Don't they understand that? For me to be so young, I had no idea that Mother Connie was that sick. I know she had her moments, but not like that. We were glad to see that Mother Connie was back on her feet to take back her life. No sickness nor death was going to keep Mother Connie down not right now. Mother Connie wasn't ready to leave yet, but she knew she wasn't in the best of health either. She continued to do what she needed to do and that was to claim her life back, so she could continue to take care of me and brother Art.

CHAPTER 8

The Lost

Did you ever have a grandmother who can sense trouble a mile away from your house, and you had no idea that it was coming your way because you were too blind to see? If anybody tell you that they knew everything that was coming their way, they lied. Tell them I said so.

A child doesn't know or see everything, and sometimes, adults don't know or see everything. I'm not saying that Grandmother Viv knew everything either, but this particular case she knew. Grandmother Viv knew when something wasn't right was coming. It was like Grandmother Viv knew something was messy. She discerned that like she know what she knew, and nobody could tell her any different. I don't believe she liked what she felt but it did seem like some trouble was coming this way.

Ask me how I know because her eyes were looking at me. There wasn't nobody else in the living room but me and her. She couldn't have been looking at the walls, not the way she was looking. No matter what trouble I was in Grandmother Viv was there. Grandmother Viv sometimes wouldn't let me go outside because of what was waiting for me. She was like a terrestrial grandmother who was there to capture you.

When the doorbell rang, it was some neighborhood friends who wanted me to go out with them. Grandmother Viv would say, "She's not going out today."

I wasn't on any punishment. She just didn't want me to go outside. I guess the world she saw, at the time, was vicious. Sometimes, the people you hang out with might have good intentions, but some of their intentions could be wrong. Your intentions could be good, but their intentions could be on a whole different level.

Grandmother Viv was a wise woman who had good sense. They looked at each other, as if to say, "What did she do now?"

I didn't do anything. It is what was waiting for me, and they couldn't even understand that. It wasn't so much of them, but an unseen force that Grandmother Viv pickup. It's not that she didn't want me to go outside; it was on that particular day. You know how these older people are. They just can't help themselves, always picking and meddling. Grandmother Viv had her moments for why she felt the way she felt. After all, she was trying to protect me and teach me the ways of the world. It took some time to catch on for what she was trying to teach me. I still had a lot of growing to do, more so she was preparing me for what was to come. I believe that's what she was doing.

Who deserve this pain in their heart? If I knew any better, I would have thought it was a hoax put on Mother Connie. I thought Mother Connie would be around forever, at least until I grow up into adulthood. You would think that everything would go as planned, right? After all, nobody is in control but the Creator. As children we would never know how our lives will end up. It was all good and perfected as I thought, but oh no! Mother Connie had to get sick again and reclaimed by God, the angels and death.

What was that all about that she had the audacity to leave all the goodness and love behind? Grandmother Viv couldn't stand the thought of losing her daughter, and her children and her brothers couldn't stand the thought of losing a sister. In the midst of all this chaos, it was too much to look at. If you would look at Mother Connie, you wouldn't think that she was sick, but can't we all say that looks are deceiving?

As time passed, I was told that Mother Connie had cancer running through her body, and that one of her lungs collapsed. What do I know all about that? I was still popping bubblegum, enjoying

Gino's fried chicken and sirloin hamburger while Mother was fighting for her life. The doctors couldn't do anything else for Mother because the cancer was already in her body, and they gave her a short time to live.

As the days were approaching, Mother Connie's sickness was aggressing; she wasn't in control this time. Grandmother Viv was making her as comfortable as she could. Grandmother Viv would cook some chicken broth soup for Mother because Mother couldn't eat nothing solid. Grandmother Viv would put a pillow behind Mother Connie's back so she could rest. I would sit and watch Mother looking at me. Mother Connie could no longer get out like she used to; she was too weak. Neighbors would visit Mother and talk to her.

In the middle of the night, me, Brother, and Grandmother would hear Mother cry and scream to the top of her lungs. While the world around us was sleeping peacefully, Grandmother Viv was up all night, taking care of her daughter because Mother was fighting the evil one out of her body. The pain Mother had to endure was a battle. Grandmother Viv would come into Mother's room to try to comfort her. Me and brother never did see the look on Mother's face because it wasn't for us to see.

The next day, I can remember Mother Connie had a good breakfast that morning. She kept us up all night long with her screaming to the top of her lungs because of the cancer in her body. Mother had eaten a big breakfast, and she didn't waste any of it. Mother Connie was sitting on the lounge chair outside on the porch, resting. I noticed Mother's legs were big. That's what it looked like to me. I said to Grandmother Viv, "Mother looks like she is gaining weight. It looks as if she is getting better."

Little that I knew about medical conditions. Mother was carrying fluid weight. In my mind, I thought Mother was getting better. For a young girl like me to think that, made me feel better to know that Mother was going to be around a long time. Grandmother Viv knew Mother was very sick, and I don't think Grandmother was ready to let her go—neither any of us was ready to let her go. Mother Connie was being prepared to go home with God. I didn't know then because I was too young to comprehend that. The Creator was ready to take Mother out of this world to be with him. I'm sure he knew that Mother suffered long enough here on this earth, and I think Mother knew that.

I don't know if Mother was scared or not. All of the sickness she had to endure, I am sure she was ready to jump out of that body of hers and fly away. That night I had slept in my bedroom—which was next to Grandmother Viv's bedroom—and Brother Art's bedroom was next to Mother Connie's bedroom. As I can remember, everything was calm with Mother. However, Grandmother would check on Mother to see if she was okay. In the early morning, Mother slipped away from this life to a new life. I woke up because the lights were on in the hallway. Grandmother Viv had said to me that Mother had died. Brother Art and I ran to Mother's room as we laid over her body and cried our hearts out so much, we couldn't stop.

While the ambulance was on the way, one of Mother's brother was there beside her, kneeling over her, weeping his heart out. Finally, the ambulance came and took Mother out of the house. Brother Art and I were sitting on Grandmother's lap, just crying all over each other, knowing that she will not wake to this life again but to a new life. Mother Connie's friends came over to the house, crying, saying, "We're going to miss Connie." That is what they called her, Connie; that was her nickname.

Oh, there was a lot of crying everywhere. They were crying all over Grandmother Viv's shoulder. Grandmother Viv was consoling them, knowing that she needed to be comforted.

Meanwhile, Grandmother Viv was preparing Mother Connie's funeral, which didn't take no time at all. Family and friends were visiting and bringing food over to the house. You can tell it was a revival in town because everybody from everywhere had brought a dish of food whenever there is a funeral or a wedding. All the invitations were written out and sent out to addresses.

The family came over, discussing what they are going to bring, so that after the funeral, we can eat. There was food everywhere. There were cakes, pies, hams, and turkeys. There was so much food. I know the people were taking a platter home. There were two grandmothers in the kitchen serving because Grandmother Viv didn't want everybody in her kitchen and some folks couldn't keep their hands clean. You have to keep your hands clean if you want to eat. Both of the grandmothers were crazy clean machines. What can I say? They were indignant when it came to their food. On that note, Grandmother Viv was deciding what dress she wanted Mother to wear. She picked out this pink dress for Mother, which looked gorgeous on Mother Connie. Whatever color she wanted to put on her daughter, it was her choice.

Finally, we were approaching to see the last time of Mother Connie. Grandmother Viv dressed me in white. I guess I had white shoes on too, white this and white that. That's what I was wearing going to the church. I couldn't understand it. That must be her favorite color. Anyway, the undertaker came and pick us up from the house to drive us to the funeral home to see Mother. There were cars everywhere, all around the corner. You would have thought Mother was celebrity. In her own right, she was.

My little friends were trampling behind me. The brothers and I were in the first car along with Grandmother. We arrived at the funeral home—that's what they called it to make you feel at home. With that being said, I will never feel the home setting because as soon as you sit down and go through all the rituals like crying and spilling out your guts, reading of the obituary and singing and getting back up to see the last of your love ones, it is time to get out of there, and be prepared for the burial. Now how much homebody is that?

We finally arrived to see Mother Connie, and what a sight to see. I looked into the casket and Mother Connie was dressed up beautifully. Her hair was to the side of her face, just like she wore her hair, and her face was gorgeous. Mother Connie looked like a star—shining bright. The family cried their hearts to pieces. I, for one, and brother, for two, couldn't stop crying. Grandmother Viv was sitting there and didn't say anything. I am sure all kinds of thoughts were going through her mind. Probably thinking what is going to become of Mother Connie's children, and how she is going to take care of us. Grandmother Viv was holding my hands, just thinking.

Mother Connie was dressed in this long pink dress with her pink pump shoes on. I believe she had a beaded necklace around her neck. The color pink was like Mother's personality—a sign of love, calming, nurturing, and perhaps an intuitive person, who doesn't pay much attention to the opinions of others. One who thinks on their own without the help of others. That's Mother for you, who doesn't care about how people think about you.

Before we knew it, the place was packed from the front to the back door. Some people had to stand against the wall. There was this man who came and stood over Mother Connie's casket and took his hat off and bowed his head in silence. I don't know if he knew Mother, but it didn't matter because it looks as if the whole world knew about Mother Connie's death. After the death of Mother Connie, nothing was the same, which was to be expected. There were times I would look in Mother's room, and look at all her things. There are other times I would walk pass and peek in her room and say, "Nope, no mother."

It happens when losing a love one. The scent of them lingers, and the thoughts of them doesn't go away—only with time. Even when the thoughts of your love ones leave your thoughts, it doesn't mean you totally forgot them. I know Mother will never be forgotten—not with me will I ever forget her. Mother Connie will be remembered and loved. I will make sure of that. I will make it my business to keep her alive in my heart, and I am sure if the tables were turned the other way around, Mother would have done the same for me. Even though she is gone, Mother, at times, pops up in my mind, remembering the times she came up to the school and gave me that look, and remembering the times she took care of me when I was sick.

CHAPTER 9

The Cleaning Lady

Meanwhile, life for us was moving swiftly. Grandmother Viv pushed Brother Art and I harder because life was approaching fast upon us. Everything around us was changing rapidly. We were growing fast. Brother Art and I had to learn quickly about the cares of this world. We both had to know about responsibilities.

Brother Art had to learn what it means to be the man of the house—not that he didn't know—besides our uncles helping out. It was three of us now since Mother was gone. Grandmother Viv believed in keeping the house clean, and she was not going to allow me and brother to lay in the bed all day long after we slept and snored all night long. She wasn't having no lazy behind children laying in the bed all day long, knowing there was a lot of work to be done. Grandmother Viv had to show brother and I what it means to have chores and be responsible, and that meant keeping the house clean and keep ourselves in check. It went on until brother was mature enough to go away in the Navy.

This was how the house should look like—clean. Every other Saturday, we had to clean house because this is the way it had to be done. Grandmother Viv had taught us swiftly of staying ahead of things. I would hear this loud noise coming into my room, waking me up out of my beauty sleep. I was somewhat in a middle of a dream, trying to finish the dream to the end, until Grandmother Viv started to run this loud vacuum cleaner into my bedroom. Doesn't she understand that you don't wake nobody out of their sleep while dreaming? That could have been a revelation for her.

Well, evidently the vacuum cleaner had no name on it. So I guess I had to be the first one to use it. She couldn't care less about how I felt. The room had to get clean. This is what she did. She came in my room, saying, "You are not going to sleep in the bed all day when there is work to be done." What gave Grandmother Viv that idea anyway? Because my intention wasn't to stay in the bed all day long. You know I like to rip and run the streets. Didn't she know that? She should have known that I would get the work done, then hit the streets.

I could remember this blue rug in my room I had to clean. She made sure that I was going to clean this rug. She dropped the vacuum cleaner on the floor; she didn't lay it down, Grandmother Viv dropped it, and said, "Finish the work," and I had to do just that.

Grandmother Viv said to Brother Art, "Go around to the corner store, and pick up half a gallon of milk, so we can have breakfast." The store Brother Art had gone to, he started working there. It was a husband-and-wife business. They just adored brother. Life was moving fast upon him. I watched how he grew into a fine gentleman. He met a beautiful young lady, who he grew to love, and she, as well, loved brother. It was called young love.

You know how it is when meeting someone, you get butterflies in your stomach, and you get starry eyes? Before his young love came along his side, there were other young girls who liked Brother Art, but Brother Art knew what he liked. You see, Brother Art knew how to get them, and he also knew if they were serious. He would play with them. He would take them out on a date, but he knew they were not his life partners.

Do you remember the clubs inside of the hotels and the DJ would take his magical fingers and move the records with his hands and it sounded like the record was scratching? Then on top of that, the DJ would play the slow jams, the oldies but the goodies—that's what it was called. I can recall me and a neighborhood friend had gone to the night club at the Holiday Inn Hotel. The club was packed out. Both of us had to stand up against the wall. However, this girl was standing next to me, and we spoke, then she had asked me, "How is your brother doing? He so fine."

How in the world did she know me and brother? Because I had no idea of who she was. I guess it is well to be expected for her to know Brother because he was popular with the girls. They must have tracked and stalked him down because they sure love them some bow legs. Brother Art is a fine son of a gun. All I can say is that Brother Art had it going on with the girls. He hooked that thing up. Do you hear what I said? Brother was grooving with the ladies, and they probably thought that he was the one for them. You have to understand that it is only one man to a woman that's only if your electrical wires in your brain are electrifying, right.

On the other hand, Grandmother Viv was on a kick of keeping everything together with me and Brother. I don't think she was too concerned about him, not in a way she was concerned about me being a girl. Brother Art was growing into a man doing his thing. Grandmother Viv was concerned about me probably because Mother had left us and knowing a girl needs their mother, and so does boys. It was her way of showing her protection.

Yes or No

The neighborhood was changing and some of the neighbors had died or have gone back to their hometown, but there were still a lot of us left. Grandmother Viv was still giving me and Brother training lessons, and those lessons she was giving us was like a marriage for a lifetime. Grandmother Viv was like a stern soldier in the army, who likes to give orders without wearing a uniform. When you thought you learned one thing, here comes something else to learn.

Usually in the neighborhood, someone likes to give trips whether to an amusement park or to the beach. At this particular time, someone was giving a trip to this particular beach, which would be a fun trip to go to. Grandmother Viv didn't think it was such a fun trip for Brother and I to go to. Brother Art and I beg her to let us go on this trip, and she said no. We were on our knees, begging Grandmother, saying, "Please. Pretty please, Grandmother. Let us go. It would be so nice for us."

Brother Art and I said to her, "Why can't we go? We're not going to get into any trouble." The answer was still no, but we were persistent on asking her, and she still said no. When Grandmother meant no, she meant no. I don't really think if it had anything do with us getting into any trouble. I think Grandmother Viv wanted to show me and Brother that an answer will not be a *yes* all the time in her vocabulary. There were times we just don't need an answer as to why. It was her way to teach us obedience and to see if we can except a *no* and not a *yes* all the time.

Brother Art and I learned about a *no* very quickly. If we didn't get the message then, we got it later. It wasn't that Grandmother didn't want us to live our lives either because she made sure that we would have plenty other opportunities that would come our way.

CHAPTER 10

The Knowing

Because of all life experiences Grandmother Viv had to encounter, especially losing her daughter, everything was heartbreaking for her. Grandmother Viv was a woman of integrity and optimism. She was determined to make sure life wasn't going to kill me and Brother Art. Grandmother Viv was the mother who was standing on the frontline for her children, who knew a lot of stuff. I am talking about stuff I thought that I could see and didn't see it coming.

Grandmother Viv was skeptical about the friends I was hanging out with. She knew the type of people I should be with and the type of people I shouldn't be with. It was like she was in control of everything. It wasn't too much I could get away with, not with her. One thing about Grandmother Viv was she didn't like gossip because she knew what it could do to a person's character.

She was upset about the mess that went down in front of her house. Me and a neighbor were sitting outside on our steps, minding our own business until some girls wanted to come to our front door and start some trouble. But why? I knew who they were, and so did the neighbor. Both of us were sitting on the steps, talking and laughing, but these were the same girls who pretended that thcy liked you. When you are young, you have misunderstandings and hope to make up. Not these girls. They wanted to fight, and it wasn't the neighbor they wanted to fight. They wanted to fight me because it was a setup, you hear me?

It wasn't that person they were after. It was me. But check this out. It was on like popcorn. What goes around must come back around. It was on, and we were ready for them. Earlier, I said, "Mother Connie knew who her true friends are and Grandmother Viv knew who her true friends are." I had to find out the long, hard way. That is why we have mothers and grandmothers, who are like soldiers in the army, to help these babies along the way without wearing a uniform. I know what I know now, you learn as you grow. Some people never learn it.

Stop Gossiping

In the summertime, Grandmother Viv would have her windows open, and she could hear everything from the front steps to the corner, and I believe around the corner of the block, that is if her antennas are way into the heavens. I guess that is the purpose of having windows, so you can open them up to get some fresh air or hear the naysayers.

Grandmother Viv was the type of woman who liked peace. She didn't like trouble because if trouble came knocking at her door, she would tell you about it. Grandmother Viv had her issues, but her issues weren't crap. Don't bring trouble to her home if you can't finish it. When you are stepping into someone else's territory to fight or go to war, prepare yourself. You don't know what might fly out the windows.

Grandmother Viv and the neighbor heard all of the noise outside of the house. They thought it was a riot outside. It was about to go down to the ground. I know they didn't think we were going to back down from them because we were ready. We were not looking for any trouble. Their troubling spirit was looking for me. I said it was me because of the looks on their faces. They thought I was going to be alone, and the neighbor was outside with me. They were in a state of shock. These sad-looking girls, who needed help, wanted to fight me. How in the world would you come to somebody's house, looking like you want to fight and couldn't fight?

Grandmother Viv knew trouble was coming this way. That is why she didn't want me to go too far from the house. The decent thing they should have done was to comb their hair. Their hair didn't look like it was done in a few days.

Will you please give me a break! Grandmother Viv wouldn't have mine doing the girls hair. She knew how to do hair. Grandmother would have hook the sista' up. In addition, Grandmother heard all this noise outside of the window, and so did the neighbor. They couldn't believe what they were hearing. They both yelled out their windows, saying, "Hey, what is going on out there? Go back to where you came from!"

They have said some words out their mouth that would have turn the city up-side-down. Brother Art must have heard the rumbling too because he ran outside with his bow-legged self, telling us to get them, they can't beat y'all. He scared them off the block, cracking up. Grandmother Viv was so upset and told us to come in the house. I said to Grandmother, "We didn't do anything. They came to start trouble with us."

We both went to the kitchen to receive counseling from Grandmother. She said, "I told you to leave those gossiping girls alone, all that 'he said, she said' stuff is enough to kill ya."

By the time Grandmother Viv left her mark on me, it was all over with and things began to change. How about that? You can't keep falling into the same thing over and over again unless you are blind and dumb. When Grandmother Viv spoke those words out of her mouth, I saw change. Everybody was splitting up. What could I say about that? I couldn't challenge her on that situation. I had to take note of the warnings. Brother Art was getting his thrill ride off that because he knew how some of the neighborhood girls were nothing that he wanted to get involve with as far as his future wife was concerned. The kitchen was like a counseling session. Everything happened in the kitchen. If you were not eating in the kitchen, you're getting your hair done, or you were getting lectured for something you did or something someone else had done. The task that Grandmother had to carry wasn't easy because she had a boy and a girl to raise.

The Journey

Moreover, Brother Art was growing fast and steady into a man, and he was making his own decisions into what he wanted to do with his life. He had his share of disappointments. However, he soared right above and beyond it. Brother Art had hopes and dreams which the Lord helped him to fulfill them. His life transitioned more and more into a responsible man. He decided to go into the Navy, and do something with his life because the streets were not giving him the opportunity that he needed and wanted. It was hard to see him go but he had to follow the path that was best for him. Brother Art made the best decision for himself.

The neighborhood was constantly changing. There were some neighbors on the block that had moved. Things were turning around, probably for the better. I already changed schools for a better education. Grandmother Viv and I continue to thrive through this journey called life. Grandmother Viv made sure that my life was to stay on track. My life had gone the way it had to go, whether I understood it or not. I know Grandmother wanted what was best for me, and she got somewhat something out of me. She made it her business that I get grades that was going to take me to the next level and finish school. Grandmother Viv saw that because every report card that was handed to me by the teacher, Grandmother had to sign it. She wasn't playing that trick, so now I know.

In this school that I was attending, we had to do a project and the assignment was to build a doll house. I didn't know anything about building a dollhouse, but that was okay because I knew Grandmother's helping hands were going to help me. I said to Grandmother, "I have a dollhouse that I have to build, and I am in a competition with all these other kids who are building a project. I need help."

Grandmother Viv and I had a cardboard box and started to put the dollhouse together. The dollhouse was three stories high, so she cut out some pieces of rug she had around the house, and I had some dolls and furniture to add to the rooms. We cut out the windows for each floor of the house. It was all coming together. Grandmother

Viv was adding her touches to it. She was having more fun than me. Her hands were all in it. The dollhouse was finally finished, and we had to wait and find out who was the winner. When Grandmother and I walked into the basement of the school, there were winners all around us. We saw all the dollhouses and other projects that were in winning mode. Grandmother Viv reminded me not to get caught up in who is in first place. It was going to be alright. It was easy for her to say that, but I was hoping I would be in first place or second place but not third or fourth place. To be honest with you, I didn't know what darn place I was in, but in a place where I did receive a grade to the next level. That was alright with me and Grandmother. All I know that everything we do in life is not all the time in first place. The winning is when you don't give up, but keep pushing forward. That is what I have done—keep moving forward. I tried not to give up on anything I put my hands to do. However, the building of the dollhouse was a process and the rest is history.

Moreover, I could recall Grandmother Viv loved to surprise me with one of her specialties and that was her meat pie dish that she loved to bake. Before I could leave out for school, Grandmother would say to me, "When you come home from school, I have a surprise for you."

I already knew what it was—one of her favorite meat pie dishes that I love for her to make from scratch. There were several times she would bake that dish for me until she got sick. This was the first time I had ever seen Grandmother get sick. Even though Grandmother recovered from her sickness, the doctors said, "Grandmother Viv had colon cancer."

Now, what kind of mess is that? First, it was Mother with lung cancer, now Grandmother with colon cancer. You got to be kidding me? It looked as if Grandmother Viv was in the hospital forever. She was supposed to be healthy, not sick.

Finally, Grandmother Viv came home, looking like she got it together. If you wanted to know anything about prayer, her sister was a praying woman who came over to our house and prayed through our home. Any time a woman like that prays, you better be ready for the countdown because she is coming to destroy whatever that is not right in the house.

I could remember Grandmother Viv would pray with me. She would make me pray the Lord's Prayer. I would look at her like what? Grandmother Viv would say, "Repeat after me."

I had no other choice but to be obedient because that tone of voice of hers would put you on your knees. The prayer had to be in my heart for real, for real. No one could take her place because Grandmother was like a woman of steel. Her sister I called the prayer warrior because she knew how to chop down stuff. This aunt of ours knew how to throw it down.

Grandmother Viv started to get better when she stopped smoking and started to eat everything like she used to. She was making those meat pies again. Oh, how I loved that because she was not leaving me! Grandmother Viv was herself again. Things started to come back together again. The old girl was back on track.

As time was moving, I was maturing, growing, and moving forward into this young girl stage. I guess that's what you want to called it. The older people called it feeling yourself, you know, liking boys. Grandmother Viv knew I was getting to that stage because she has been there and done that. Oh yeah, the boys. I said things were swiftly changing—boy liking girl, girl liking boy. Grandmother Viv wanted to talk to me about the boys, about the birds and the bees. The birds and the bees, I wasn't trying to hear that. It was a saying that the older people used to say. She made it clear to me about everything.

So, here I was, sitting near the window in her room, which you could see everything. Grandmother Viv was sitting on her bed, looking at me with her deep dark eyes. Her eyes were too deep for me. She could look right through you, like a sword piercing your heart. She wasn't no joke. I would say to her, "Grandmother what is wrong? What?" Grandmother Viv would say to me, "I know you're liking the boys but be careful." What could I say but look and listen to her. She was putting it on me because of that time of my life.

It's about Time

We finally heard from Brother Art. Where in the world has he been? He finally came back to reality. I guess overseas made him into a real man. Grandmother Viv would get letters from Brother, then he would start writing to me. Me and brother would go back and forth writing each other letters. My heart was full of joy to hear from him. He would say to me that I write beautiful letters. However, there were times brother would write to me and started preaching to me about my life and what the Bible says about salvation.

Okay here we go again about the Bible. Could we just talk about other things like my beautiful handwriting? Brother Art was going on about this salvation thing, but he was serious. He wanted to make sure that I wasn't going to be swallowed up with the cares of this world. Brother Art knew that I wasn't seeing right with his eye-seeing self. Okay, does anybody see right in their beginning stages in life? I am not trying to see right, only for what I want to see. On my side of the fence, I didn't say that to him because he probably would have snatched me far distance. I had never seen anybody so fired up like him. He would go on and on, writing me letters about what the Lord said. I heard you, Brother, but it didn't mean I was ready. I had some living to do of my own. Do you get that brother? Or can you hear that? You see, Brother was ready to settle down with a family, but me, myself, and I were still in searching mode.

Someday, I would turn about-face when time was of essence. Brother Art was intuitive to both worlds because he lived in that world that turn against him, until that world shattered and he turned about-face to the heavens. That was why he wanted me to turn around because that world would soon turn against me. What a wise man. He had no doubt in his mind that me and the family would turn it over to the Most High God because his faith was that strong.

Moving Forward

Meanwhile, I was coming to an end of the eighth grade, and my graduation was approaching. Grandmother Viv, and I was excited because this chapter was closing in my life. Yeah, I was happy but sad at the same time. I knew I wasn't going to see my good old classmates, to whom we grew to be a family. The teachers and the classmates had gone through some tough times together, which made us appreciate one another even the more, and not to take each other for granted. We said our goodbyes, hugs, and kisses. Graduation was finally here, and Grandmother Viv and her sons and other family members came to this big day for me to graduate.

Usually on graduation day, the students would sit on the end sit, so when their names are called, they could get up and receive their awards. When my name was called to come up, my homeroom teacher and I stood face-to-face and cried, and she told me that she was going to miss me. She knew the struggles I had went through, but came out of them all. After graduation was over, we went back to our daily lives. Who would have thought that after you close one chapter of your life, another chapter would open? But not in a sense that it would have been disturbing.

When I looked at Grandmother Viv, I see her as one who could lead an army, and that she did in our family—a woman who was beat down by life problems, who stood the test of time of losing her daughter. That's a big gulp right there. Then, she had to turn around and bury another child? Losing one child puts a hole in your heart, but losing two children can put a person in their grave.

She wasn't the only affected by it. The whole family was at a loss for words. What could you say when you are lost for words? Grandmother Viv was out of it. She was done. Life wasn't life to her anymore after losing two children and only have one more left. Nope, Grandmother Viv wasn't going to bury her last child. That was not on her agenda. She made sure of that. If anything, her last child was going to bury her, and that he did.

Grandmother Viv wasn't trying to hear nothing about death, burial, and grave. I was already in high school, being challenged to do my very best because that is what Grandmother wanted from me.

After her son died, who she loved dearly, I started noticing how Grandmother wasn't doing so well with her health. Maybe she felt life didn't treat her right, and maybe it didn't treat her nicely. When she lost both of her children, I believe Grandmother wanted to give up because that had to leave a hole in her heart and feeling separated from her children. No one could understand that unless they had to experience it themselves. Sister girl is not making any suggestions or giving any advice. I'm just making a point. No parent should go through that trauma because it's a big one.

CHAPTER 11

The Last Days

Grandmother Viv was one who knows how life can throw a curve ball and continued to go about her daily life and lived. I continued to do what I needed to do and that was to finish school. The family came over to see us more because Grandmother was getting worst by the days, weeks, and months. I can't even imagine living my life without this precious woman, knowing that things were changing fast.

I can recall her being so sick, and I laid in bed with her that night because I needed to be next to Mommy. How can a child keep going through that? It was one thing after another. That night, I laid on Grandmother's chest, it was too much to bear. It was the most comforting thing for me to do. Grandmother needed to know that she wasn't alone. Whatever she was going through in her darkest moments, I was experiencing my darkest moment as well. We both were experiencing our days out together. I laid there and cried on her chest, knowing that this was our last days together, so I had to make the best of it. When Grandmother Viv had asked me, "What are you going to do when I am gone?"

I said to her, "I don't know. What I am going to do?"

All I know was that the tears were pouring down my face like an overflowing river that couldn't be stopped. I cried myself to sleep, hoping that this was only a dream, realizing the next morning was the same thing. Grandmother Viv was still in the same state she was in from yesterday. While I was in Science class, I asked the teacher if there were anything that could cure Grandmother's disease. Hopefully, I would get an answer, knowing that maybe something the class was studying would bring a healthy response to the questionable state I was encountering. The science teacher knew I had questions about this deadly disease, but she had to be honest and tell me an answer that I didn't want to hear..

It was my last days with Grandmother because she was in preparation to leave me. I continued to focus on finishing school to learn and to grow. Even though challenges and oppositions were facing me, I had to keep focus as far as my eyes could see.

Grandmother Viv was admitted to the hospital, and her last days were approaching. Brother Art came home on leave from the Navy because of the call he received that Grandmother Viv wasn't doing too well. It was so good to see brother looking sharp in his uniform. As I walk into the hospital, all I felt was sickness and me crying, then I walked into Grandmother's room. I looked at her and said to her, "Are you going to die?"

Oh, what did I say that for? And I had no clue about what she said but she looked at me. Her sister was there, the one who I said was a prayer warrior and that she was. I was hoping that Auntie Prayers would heal Grandmother's sickness. Oh no. Auntie saw that I needed to be prayed for because I had a long journey ahead of me.

Brother Art and I were in his room, standing near his dresser, and a mirror above it. The sorrow that I felt was that Grandmother Viv was no longer with us. The grief of it all was too much to bare. I could remember brother consoling me to let me know everything was going to be alright. Uncle was in so much turmoil, being the last child, trying to hold everything together. It was a living nightmare for him, losing his sister, brother, and mother. He was upset because I asked Grandmother Viv if she was going to die. The only way he knew was that Grandmother told him. I was sure she had every right to ask him that question or however that story played out.

Hey now, I had no other way to release what I was feeling but to ask her about her leaving me. It was on my heart, so I asked her was she going to die. Maybe that was a hard pill to swallow to ask someone that question. The question had to come out, and the answer wasn't coming fast enough. I needed answers quick, and everybody seemed to be in their own little world with no care in the world.

Besides me finishing school, I needed to know which way my life was turning—for the bad, good or for the worst. Some people probably didn't think that was appropriate thing to say. So, what was appropriate and inappropriate? Okay, you can't answer the question, so let's move on.

Brother Art knew I had a long journey ahead of me, and it wasn't going to be an easy one. The journey was going to be a long one. After the death of Grandmother Viv, I saw how my world turned upside-down, inside out and all around and about. I know that's a mouthful right there. Bother Art had my back. He prayed for me and continued to write me letters. He prayed for me until my world came back on track. Because of the prayers going up, it didn't take that long.

Moreover, Grandmother Viv was dressed in this beautiful powder blue dress, and her hair was made up like the picture I saw of her to her shoulders. No more pain or suffering in this world. The world she entered into was nothing like this world. She was resting in the arms of her Savior. It was a big loss because Grandmother kept everyone together. She was the matriarch of the family, and I can say that she left her mark. She made sure of that. As for me, life was changing, but in a way that I didn't expect it to be, in a way that God intended it to be. Even though I had to face some challenges to get me through, I continued to stay focused as healing was taken place in my life.

I am sure there are others that can say the same thing. When life hits you hard, you're going to do everything in your strength not to go down. And if you do go down, you can pick yourself back up and keep on running. As far as my eyes could see, I didn't know how life was going to turn out for me, but I had to keep the faith in knowing that the world I live in was not going to put me in my grave at an early age. I was determined to win and not give up. It wasn't easy, but it wasn't too bad either because I had people in my life to help me through this journey.

I had to learn differently in order to see differently. I know there are a lot of people that life hit them hard. Some made it through, some didn't, but it's not for me to judge of who got through this thing called life because I know the Creator helped me and kept me from losing it. It wasn't anything that I was looking for to happen in my life. It was something that I just couldn't explain and only ask the question why I had to go through this thing.

We all have our crosses to bear but some of us have it harder than others. I happen to be the one who had to go through the school of hard knocks at an early age, and didn't have any conscious thought of how I was going to come out of it. There are times that we go through traumas and don't have a clue as to how we are going to come out of this living nightmare we have to deal with on Earth. All I know is if Job had to go through his test and trials and the Lord had to go through his test and trials, then I guess I had to be the one to go through my test and trial at an early age and come out on the winning side.

I don't have a formula as to how I pass through this death situation, only to know that I had caring people who prayed for me, and gave me hope that my life was not the end but the beginning. And to know that God has a plan for my life, and it is not finished until God says it is finished.

ABOUT THE AUTHOR

Dolores V. Randall was born and raised in Philadelphia, Pennsylvania on a block called 61st Street where it all began and ended but not her life. She played sports such as basketball girls' team, which was called 20th century sports at a team center in West Philadelphia. She also ran track and did some flips and dips while doing gymnastics. While working at Thomas Jefferson University Hospital, she attended night school September of 1991 part-time to receive her associate degree in general studies. She completed her courses and graduated. Later, she took a course in medical assistance and received her certification. She went back to school to get a bachelor degree of science in urban ministry leadership at Lancaster Bible College, Center for Urban Theological Studies (CUTS). Most of all, she likes traveling and do what she likes to do.